Boko Haram and the Chibok Girls: A Common Guilt is all We Share

N.I.O. and D.L-B.

Introduction

When we set out to write a tell-all book on the Boko Haram sect, we had no illusions. We knew that writing this book would place the writers at risk but this did not deter us from carrying out this project. We just had to write the book for two compelling reasons. First, we had inside information that many other people did not have and it was important to pass this information to the world. Second, there was a lot of misconception about this deadly sect. It is possible that the sect had a media section that was bent on misinforming the world. Well, we could not allow the myths and the half-truths to continue to thrive. Since we knew the truth about this criminal organization, we felt duty bound to make this information available to the world.

We are happy to state that the project has been a successful one so far. The small book "Boko Haram: Between Myth and Reality" has been very well received by the reading public. People from different parts of the globe have commended the writers of this book and some of the reviews have been truly amazing. The only complaint so far is that the writers did not quote sources and the book had very few footnotes. Well, we have to take this criticism in good faith but we can as well use this opportunity to point out that our hands were tied.

We were working on a relatively dangerous project and one of the writers still lives in northern Nigeria. This is the BH territory so there was no need to put this writer's life at risk. More to the point, there was no reason to quote sources if mentioning those people in the book would endanger their lives. Finally, there is the frequently overlooked fact that some of the incidents described in the book were eye-witness accounts. Pray, if you have witnessed an event, why would you have any need to "quote your sources?" These are some of the dilemmas we faced at the time and this is why we carefully avoided mentioning sources by name.

In this new book though, we have found a way to get around this problem. We are going to quote some of our sources but we shall do so in a safe manner. The war against insurgency is still raging in the three states of Borno, Yobe and Adamawa. Even as we write, the three states are still under emergency rule but we are optimistic that the federal government troops will win the war. To paraphrase the immortal words of Dennis Brutus; "Peace will return and men will go home".

N.I.O. and D.L-B.

Contents

Chapter 1
Day one: The Kidnapping of the Chibok School Girls

On April 14 2014, a particular government official in Chibok, Borno state received a phone call. His caller had been calling for a while without getting through. When he finally got through, it was clear that the man was agitated. A large convoy of Boko Haram fighters was advancing to Chibok. He had it on good authority that these fighters were going to kidnap girls in a particular secondary school. He was therefore calling the said government official to alert the Joint Military Task Force stationed in the area so that the BH fighters would be stopped from carrying out this deadly mission.

In fairness to the government official, this man tried his best. He promptly called a hotline and got through immediately. The person he called was a soldier and a member of the Joint Task Force. The government official passed on the information he had just received and added that the soldiers in the area should hurry to prevent the kidnapping. The soldier made a few calls of his own and promptly mobilized his men. It is on record that an attempt was made to thwart the Boko Haram attack but the soldiers were outnumbered, outgunned and outmaneuvered. The soldiers beat a hasty retreat and the BH convoy proceeded unhindered all the way to Government Girls Secondary School, Chibok.

It is important to point out at this point that the Government Girls Secondary School, Chibok had been shut down in March, 2014. Since September 2013, the BH had been busy burning schools, shooting students and conscripting some high school students into their army. The state government could no longer guarantee the safety of the students so all the high schools in the state were shut down. In the aftermath of the kidnapping of the Chibok girls, the military claimed they had no idea that some schools in the state had been reopened. We will get back to this point later, but let us look at the anatomy of the kidnapping of those school girls first.

Anatomy of the kidnapping

When the BH troops got to the school, it was late at night and most of the girls were preparing to go to bed. Some of the girls were still awake studying for the next day's papers. They had just written Biology and were supposed to write Literature-in-English the next day. The BH fighters went straight to the hostels and forced their way into the dormitories. At this point, the girls were not worried. The BH troops were dressed in military uniforms and some of their trucks were painted in military colors. Their spokesman informed the students that the school was 'in danger of attack by militants, and the Nigerian army had sent them to rescue the students and take them to a safe location.' The girls believed this story and entered the trucks and buses of their own volition. It was only after the "soldiers" started chanting "Allahu Akbar" that the girls began to suspect that something was seriously wrong. Their worst fears were confirmed when some of the "soldiers" began setting the school ablaze. At this point, some of the students made a dash for freedom and succeeded. Most of them were too frightened to react so they remained in the trucks and hoped for a miracle.

The BH fighters took their time to burn most of the hostel to the ground. They also had time to carry out an unsuccessful search for the few brave girls who had elected to vote with their feet. When the search for these girls proved unsuccessful, the convoy with hundreds of teenage girls, left the school and began the long journey to the Sambisa forest. Mid way into the journey, one of the trucks broke down. Apparently the BH fighters had their own in-house mechanic. While this mechanic was fixing the truck, a few other girls jumped off the truck and disappeared into the night. By now, some of the BH fighters were rattled. Their orders were to bring the girls alive and well into the Sambisa forest and not to shoot the ones trying to escape. But they could not quietly watch their captives disappear into the night so they hurriedly repaired the truck and drove off at top speed.

Too many unanswered questions

Now, there are many questions begging for answers here. First, the Borno state government had ordered the closure of all secondary schools in the state and the order was carried out. Who gave the order for the re-opening of the school in Chibok? Why was the school re-opened? The first question has remained unanswered but there is a simple answer to the second one. According to a teacher in the school who spoke to one of the writers, technically, the school was not re-opened. The thing is that the final year students were due to write the West African School Certificate Examination. Their colleagues in other states were writing the exams already so somebody decided that it would not be right for the students to miss out on this exam after six years of secondary education. But who told the students to return to school? The teacher stated bluntly that he knew but would not disclose.

The security question

When the BH started attacking high schools in Borno, the government deployed soldiers to provide security in some of the schools that were at risk. How come there were no security men to protect Government Girls Secondary School, Chibok? We posed this question to a government official who initially stated that he was not competent to speak on the matter. We asked him to refer us to an official who "is competent to speak on the matter". The answer he gave us was a classic exercise in sophistry and we can quote his statement in full. "My friend, the school was not officially open and you know it. How do you expect anybody to apply for security in a school that is officially closed? Answer me that one." Of course, we could not "answer him that one" so we let him off the hook.

The response of the military before and after

Considering the response of the Nigerian military, (or the lack of response) it is fair to state that the soldiers in Borno did not exactly cover themselves in glory:

Fact number 1. The soldiers knew of the attack hours before it took place and yet they did not do enough to stop it.

Fact number 2. The BH insurgents took their sweet time to round up the girls, burn down the school and drive off with the girls.

How come a military action was not mounted to rescue the girls immediately? The BH militants even had time to repair their truck and yet they were not pursued by the military. Meanwhile, Borno state was already under a state of emergency. The poor response by the military gave the opposition a lot of ammunition to attack Nigerian soldiers and the federal government in the aftermath of the kidnapping of those girls. We shall get to this later but now let us look at the reactions of some Nigerians to the most audacious kidnapping saga in the history of the country.

Chapter 2

Day Two: Fear, Shock and Anxiety

The Ika people of Delta state in Nigeria's south-south region have a saying to the effect that the news you receive in the dead of the night cannot be considered authentic until you have verified it in the light of day. This aphorism is applicable to the situation in Chibok and neighboring areas in the early hours of April 15, 2014.

From the night of April 14 to the early hours of April 15, telephone lines in Chibok and elsewhere had been ringing non-stop. Many people in Chibok and the nearby areas of Askira, Damboa and Biu were aware that the Boko Haram sect had "done something" in the Government Girls Secondary School in Chibok. However, most people did not know the details but they feared that the worst had happened. In the lexicon of Borno and Yobe states, the expression "the BH has done something" usually means suicide bombing, a shooting spree or a bit of beheading. The BH at this time was not known for large scale kidnapping of teenage girls. This is the precise reason many people doubted the kidnap story. By noon on April 15, some of the girls who escaped had arrived home in Chibok. These girls gave graphic accounts of what happened the previous night and they were promptly spirited away to other cities in case the BH foot soldiers came looking for them.

Initial Reactions to the Kidnapping

Chibok is one of the few places that can be considered a Christian enclave in Borno state. The people here had bluntly refused to convert to Islam during the days of the Sokoto Jihad and the El Kanemi movement. Those who were already practicing traditional African religion back then did not see why they should accept "this new Arab religion". When Christianity came to the old Borno region, the Chibok were among the first converts in the whole region. As a result, they worked closely with the British missionaries and many of them joined the clergy. Another result of early conversion to Christianity was that the Chibok people got western education pretty early. Today, they are easily the most well educated people in the old Borno state. Many of them are professionals and technocrats playing important roles in the civil service, in private business and in the professions. Qualified and competent Chibok professionals can be found in the big cities of Lagos and Abuja where they hold important positions. Unfortunately, back home in Borno, they are not appreciated. They were considered "uppity and educated minority Christians" who were not loyal (read subservient) to the Shehu of Borno and other Emirs in different parts of the state. To cut the story short, many Chibok Christians, like other Christians in Biu, Askira and Damboa were discriminated against on the grounds that they were not "fellow Muslims".

The Kidnapping as an Anti-Christian Agenda

According to Joseph Barka in Chibok; "There are many secondary schools in this state. Now, ask yourself this question. Why is it that the one place with a large population of Christian girls in the whole state is the one that was targeted by the BH. This is a confirmation of everything we have been saying all along. Boko Haram is a northern Muslim agenda against the Christians in the north of this country. I have said this before and I will say it again. But the Almighty God is on our side and he will not forsake his people".

You may consider the words of Mr. Joseph the opinion of an aggrieved Christian but it was not the only popular opinion on the day. From the Borno state capital in Maiduguri, (80 miles away) a Muslim Cleric gave his own opinion. "The Boko Haram people are not in the habit of kidnapping little girls. This is NOT the work of Boko Haram and people should not keep blaming them for what they did not do. There is no proof that they did this and I challenge anybody who is accusing them to come out and give us evidence or keep quiet. Also, people should not keep on wiping (whipping up) religious sentiments. These people are not attacking only Christians. They are attacking everybody in Nigeria. They are killing both Muslim and Christian and they are killing both the Sarauta (royalty) and the Talakawa (masses)".

In the town of Chibok, Mrs. Ladi Ndiribula (not her real name) whose three daughters were among those unaccounted for could not eat or sleep since hearing the sad news. "I am not interested in who carried out the act and who did not carry out the act. I just want my girls to come home. That is all I want. Their father is dead and my son and my daughters are all I have in this world. I want my daughters to come home."

Response by the Police and the Army

One of the most terrible things about the kidnapping of the Chibok girls was the response (or lack of response) by the military and police authorities. Now, it is possible that the police had not finished carrying out investigations on April 15, 2014. This is probably why they could not say anything on the day. It is also possible that military policy prevented the soldiers on the ground from making statements until they had cleared things with their bosses in Abuja. This is understandable because there was a war going on and there was no point in rushing off to make statements without having all the facts. This is why what happened on April 16, 2014 was simply inexplicable.

Chapter 3

Day Three: False Information from the Military High Command

On the day the Chibok girls were kidnapped, the most senior officer on the ground was Lt. Col. A.O. Ojo. To be fair to this officer, he was not stationed in Chibok but he did not have to be. As the Unit Commander in the military formation in nearby Biu, Chibok was under his jurisdiction. In effect, 2nd Lieutenant V.I. Godknows, the only commissioned officer in Chibok on April 14, 2014 reported directly to Lt. Col. A.O. Ojo. Note that Capt. O.O. Ogunrinde was also posted to Chibok officially. For some unexplained undisclosed reasons, this officer was not in Chibok on the day the girls were kidnapped. All three officers (along with 13 other enlisted men) were later court-martialed by the army but this would be months after they had embarrassed the nation.

The Crime-in-Chief of the Lt. Colonel was that he Gave Wrong Information to his Superior Officers.

On April 16 2014, it was clear that students, hundreds of students, had been kidnapped from the Government Girls Secondary School, Chibok. It was also clear that some of these girls escaped from their captors. The truth is that, at this point, nobody knew exactly how many girls were kidnapped. Lt. Col. A.O. Ojo was the ranking officer in Chibok so it was his duty to brief his bosses on the situation on the ground. According to this officer, about 100 girls were abducted but most of them had returned home. He did not mention the exact number of girls kidnapped. He did not disclose the number of those who escaped nor did he state how these girls escaped. Contrary to information published by some media houses at the time, this officer did not claim or imply that his boys rescued the girls who had returned home. He simply reported to his bosses that some girls were kidnapped and that most of them had escaped. This was the statement issued by the army spokesman and this statement caused considerable outrage in Chibok and other parts of Borno state.

Fortunately, the principal of the school, Mrs. Asabe Kwambura was not part of this misinformation plot. She bluntly stated that hundreds of her girls were missing. For good measure, she brought out school records to back up her claims. From the information made available by this lady, it became clear that close to 300 girls were kidnapped on April 14. About 53 of these girls managed to escape in batches so over 200 girls were still in captivity.

After this disclosure by the Principal, the army was forced to retract the earlier statement and the brick bats began to fly.

The Kidnapping as an Opportunity for the Blame Game

One terrible thing about Nigerian politicians is that they try to make political capital out of every situation. This misfortune of the Chibok girls (like the attack on the World Trade Center in New York) should have been an opportunity for the politicians to close ranks and fight a common enemy. Instead these leaders saw the kidnapping as a perfect opportunity to trade blame.

The APC Accusation

The opposition All Progressives Congress (APC) fired the first salvo. This party which has many former members of the ruling People's Democratic Party (PDP) described the Jonathan regime as a clueless government. For good measure, they added that the once-respected Nigerian Army had also become clueless under the leadership of President Jonathan. An APC spokesman stated bluntly that Mr. Jonathan should not contest for a second term in office if he does not "find and rescue" the Chibok girls.

The PDP Response

This accusation stung the PDP image makers into action. One presidential spokesman accused the APC of being the political arm of Boko Haram. The spokesman in question went on to state that Nigerians are not deceived. According to this official, the unrelenting pressure on the federal government to offer amnesty to Boko Haram members was evidence of the unholy agenda of certain people from a particular part of the country.

The Asari Dokubo Theory

The most surprising theory on the kidnapping of the Chibok girls was postulated by a colorful character called El Hajj Asari Dokubo. This man is the leader of the Niger Delta Peoples Volunteer Force (NDPVV). Mujaheed Asari Dokubo is from the same Ijaw ethnic group as the president. He is a devout Muslim and has performed the pilgrimage to Makkah a number of times. He is also a former Niger Delta militant and by his own admission, he received training in Afghanistan with some present day Boko Haram fighters.

According to El Hajj Dokubo, the kidnapping of the Chibok girls was a scam. These girls were not kidnapped. They were taken away by some politicians in Borno state to discredit the government of President Goodluck Jonathan and to prevent him from contesting a second term in office. Asari berated the northern leaders who "did nothing for their people when they were in power" and advised them to return the girls they were hiding.

Chapter 4

April 17-May 04: Outrage, Intrigue and the Continuation of the Blame Game.

The announcement by the Military High Command that only "some" girls had been abducted and that most had escaped, and the retraction of that announcement gave the Nigeria Army a huge credibility problem. It also had far-reaching consequences in different parts of the country. Let us look at some of the immediate results of this unfortunate announcement by the Army spokesman and how people in the country reacted to it.

The Reaction of the Opposition

Even at the best of times, the opposition All Progressives Alliance (APC) believed that the ruling People's Democratic Party (PDP) was doing nothing. Officials of this party have used choice words like "clueless", "incompetent", "corrupt" and "daft" to describe Nigeria's president. The kidnapping of the Chibok girls, the audacious manner in which it was done, and the seeming impotence of both the army and the police, only gave the opposition more ammunition to attack the president. Some APC officials told the president to visit Chibok immediately and stop hiding in Abuja. For good measure, some of these politicians used the opportunity of this sad incident to issue threats and ultimatums. Other unpaid advisers across the land told the president to give the kidnappers whatever they wanted so that the girls would be freed.

Some retired military officers stated bluntly that "enough is enough". These "retired but not tired" officers made it clear that the army had not done enough to crush the BH. Some of them volunteered to come out of retirement and help "bomb those savages out of existence". Sadly, all this talk did nothing to address the grief, the pain and the loss of the parents of the Chibok girls. This is why some Chibok men made their own attempt to rescue their daughters.

The attempt to rescue the Chibok Girls

The first (and only) attempt to rescue the kidnapped girls was made by the Civilian Joint Task Force (JTF) and some able bodied men in Chibok. The civilian JTF is a local armed vigilant group whose members have repeatedly put their lives on the line to fight the Boko Haram. Curiously, the members of this group have succeeded in many cases where the Nigerian military have failed. Among other duties, they infiltrate the Boko Haram (probably the most dangerous job in Nigeria); gather information for the military and act on this information when the soldiers cannot or will not act on the information they have been given. This is the group of courageous men who decided to venture into the Sambissa Forest to rescue the Chibok girls. Wearing charms and protective amulets, armed with locally made rifles and clubs, this group took off in the direction of the huge Sambissa Forest. The problem is that the forest covers hundreds of kilometers. The Sambissa forest begins in Nigeria and extends to Chad, Cameroun and the Central African Republic. Since the civilian JTF did not know the exact part of the forest where the girls were being held, they had to give up after combing part of the forest without success. The point here is that they did something and they made the effort. This is more than one can say for the Nigerian military and the country's voluble politicians.

Meanwhile, some Nigerians spent the last two weeks of April defending Boko Haram. According to these avid defenders of Boko Haram, there was no proof that the kidnapping was carried out by the Jama'atu Ahlis Sunna Lidda'Awati Wal-Jihad.

Chapter 5

May 5, 2015 Shekau Claims Responsibility

On May 5, 2014, the Boko Haram leader, Imam Abubakar Shekau, decided to give Nigerians all the proof they wanted. The BH leader released a video in which he claimed credit for the kidnapping of the Chibok girls. In this video, the normally reticent Abubakar Shekau was clearly in a voluble mood.

He claimed that the young girls had no business in western schools because they were old enough to get married. He stated that he had warned northern Nigerian girls not to attend western schools but they refused to listen. He threatened to sell the girls because this is what Allah (SWT) commanded him to do. He also pointed out that Islam does not condemn slavery. According to him, the Prophet Muhammad (SAW) took slaves during the Yakin Badr (the Badr war in Hejaz region in present day Saudi Arabia). In this 57 minute video, Shekau mentioned some of his enemies like Bush, Obama and Jonathan and promised he would crush them. He also stated that the BH had friends in Afghanistan, Mali, Yemen and Pakistan.

Abubakar Shekau ended his outburst by condemning Muslim leaders in the north who he described as infidels and hypocrites. He mentioned Muslim politicians like Malam Aminu Kano, Abubakar Tafawa Balewa and Usman Dan Fodio and cursed them for betraying Islam by accepting the Nigerian constitution and operating in a democratic dispensation. He also found time to state the classic defense of Boko Haram that many BH apologists have been repeating like a mantra. "They killed Muhammad Yusuf. They killed us in Shendam (Plateau state) and they killed us in Zangon Kataf (Kaduna state)".

Chapter 6

The identity of the Chibok Girls

One immediate result of the video released by Abubakar Shekau is that for the first time, the world had a glimpse at the faces of these unfortunate girls. This video also helped the process of identifying these girls. First, a screen grab was taken from this video. This was enlarged and printed and copies were given to the police and other law enforcement agents. The Principal of the Government Secondary School in Chibok identified the girls in the video as her students. Some of the girls who had escaped tearfully identified their friends and class mates. So did the parents of these girls in Chibok and other areas. With the positive identification of these girls, some Nigerian media houses decided to publish the manes of the girls. This list of names tells its own story. Most of the girls were Christians and this is proof (if anybody ever needed proof) that the BH targeted Christian girls. It also reinforced the earlier accusation that some of the Muslim captives were allowed to escape by the BH commanders.

Chapter 7

Hopes, Dreams and Disappointments

One of the saddest things about the misfortune of the Chibok girls is that we keep hoping against hope. Alexander pope, the English poet, was spot on when he stated; "hope springs eternal in the human breast". Human beings are "hopers" because this is simply the way we are configured. Even in situations when it is clear that we may not have grounds for hope, we continue to hope. And to pray.

Ironically, our first glimmer of hope came from the statement of the army officer who told the world in the middle of April 2014 that most of the kidnapped girls "had returned home". We believed him then because this is what we wanted to hear. In any case, the BH was not known for large-scale abduction of teenage girls. Recall that some BH gunmen had abducted the elder statesman, Ali Monguno some time ago but he was released unhurt after a while. Again, it did not quite add up that Shekau and his band of bombers would like hundreds of girls to hang out in their hideouts in the Sambissa forest and elsewhere. Therefore, we put all things together and decided that the Chibok girls would be released if the government met the (anticipated) ransom demand. Unfortunately, Abubakar Shekau had other ideas.

The Obasanjo Bombshell

In the middle of June 2014, General Olusegun Obasanjo, former military Head of State and former Nigerian president released what has become known in certain quarters as the OBASANJO BOMBSHELL. The retired army officer was interviewed by the BBC Hausa Service and he expressed startling views on the Chibok girls. On June 14, 2015, The Daily Post Nigeria published excerpts of that interview and quoted Obasanjo in full.

According to the Daily Post, Obasanjo told the BBC Hausa that; ".... I believe that some of them will never return. We will still be hearing about them many years from now, some will give birth to children of the Boko Haram members, but if they cannot take care of them in the forest, they may release them".

As far as controversial statements go, this one takes the biscuit. Now, there are many questions here and most of them cannot be answered easily.

How did Obasanjo know that the Chibok girls may not all be released? How did he know that some of the girls may be pregnant from their abductors already? More to the point, what was the intention of Chief Obasanjo when he made this statement?

Well, to answer the first question, Gen. Obasanjo seemed to know what he was talking about because he admitted in the same interview that "I have ways of reaching them (Boko Haram) but I have not been given the go ahead." It is a fact that the former president had made at least one attempt to arrange negotiations between the federal government and Boko Haram leaders. In September 2011, Obasanjo travelled to Maiduguri and held a meeting with Babakura Fugu the brother-in-law of Muhammad Yusuf. Remember that both Yusuf and Baba Fugu Muhammad (Babakura's father) were executed by the police in 2009. The aim of this meeting was to convince the leadership of Boko Haram to negotiate with the federal government. Apparently, something went wrong because Babakura Muhammad was killed by the BH gunmen two days after this meeting.

The next question has to do with the allegation that some of the girls may be pregnant already and would give birth to Boko Haram children? How did His Excellency know this? It is hard to tell but one thing is clear. Obasanjo does not speak because he likes to hear the sound of his voice. Before making such a serious statement, he must have had information that other ordinary people did not have.

Finally, what was the intention of Obasanjo when he made this statement? In a land where millions of people were hoping that the Chibok girls would be released unharmed, this statement was not what people wanted to hear. So was Obasanjo indirectly sending a message to the world? Was he trying to prepare parents of the Chibok girls and other concerned Nigerians to consider the one possibility they did not even want to contemplate? The only man who can answer this question is Mathew Okikiola Olusegun Obasanjo himself. One thing is certain, though. After Obasanjo dropped this bombshell, more bad news began to make the rounds.

At this point, it is important to mention a popular Nigerian superstitious belief. In many parts of the country, local people believe that "if you say that something bad will happen, it will probably happen". This belief has been modified by Pentecostal Christians who routinely tell their members; "do not confess negative". Until Obasanjo dropped this bombshell, nobody had come out to state what we all feared might happen. It was after the publication of the Obasanjo statement that many people "started to remember things".

Ahmad Bello, a native of Kolofata in Cameroun, stated that "the girls are in Kolofata. I have seen them with my two naked eyes". Kolofata is just 15 kilometers away from the Nigerian border so it is possible that Mr. Bello knew what he was talking about. Some Fulani herdsmen in the Lake Chad border area told one of the writers of this book that they saw a large number of young girls being ferried across Lake Chad into northern Cameroun. The girls were packed into the local kwole-kwole (Hausa word for canoe) and "they looked happy". The leader of this group, Ardo Sunusi, who spoke in Fulfulde stated that he heard some girls were kidnapped but admitted that he had no way of knowing if the girls he saw in canoes were the kidnapped girls or not.

On June 25 2014, one of the writers of this book received an important phone call. The caller was Bakura, a Kanuri Muslim who does not want his surname mentioned. Bakura said that his cousin Modu had just gotten married. According to Bakura, his cousin lives in the Lake Chad area of Borno. Modu was not a BH member but he had BH connections. Apparently, he told one of his friends he was looking for a wife and this friend had found "a young and educated girl" for him. According to Bakura, Modu's bride was one of the kidnapped Chibok girls who had converted to Islam. How did he (Bakura) know this and how sure was he? Bakura replied that Modu told him and he believes that Modu told him the truth.

Chapter 8

The Bring Back Our Girls Campaign

The Bring Back our Girls (BBOG) movement s a classic irony. It started out as a truly altruistic movement. Hundreds of young Nigerian girls had been abducted from their secondary school hostels. Their only crime was that they were trying to get an education to make them better people in future. The Nigerian government that was supposed to protect these innocent girls had failed to protect them. The police and the military had six hours notice but were unable to prevent the abduction of these girls. The Nigerian army had also failed to rescue them months after their kidnap. If public institutions could do nothing for these girls, it was up to concerned private individuals to do the needful. This is the noble starting point of the BBOG movement.

Some of the brightest women in the land were part of this movement. In Abuja, the organization was represented by the one and only Obiageli Ezekwesili, chartered accountant and former minister of education. Ms Ezekwesili is a co-founder of Transparency International and a former Vice-President of the World Bank. Other leading lights of the BBOG movement are Aisha Oyebode, Yemisi Ransome-Kuti, Betty Anyanwu-Akeredolu, Amina Hanga and Eleanor Nwadinobi. The movement was an instant success and within a matter of weeks, global figures like Michele Obama, Chris Brown, Malala Yousafzai and Gordon Brown took up the cause of the BBOG movement. The Nigerian business woman and philanthropist, Modupe Ozolua flew in from the US and offered her support to the movement.

Reputable organizations like Global March Against Child Labor, Walk Free, Education International and World at School supported the movement and so did thousands of Nigerian professionals in the UK, Canada and the US. The movement held successful and well attended rallies in New York, London, Abuja, Lagos, Salt Lake City and Atlanta. There were also events in India, Pakistan and Ghana.

Unfortunately, this movement lost its credibility and its innocence when its members began to hang out with the wrong crowd. The first sign of trouble came from unlikely quarters. A distinguished member of this movement urged the president, Mr. Goodluck Jonathan, to "release the kidnapped girls from Aso Rock". The message here is that President Jonathan is complicit in the abduction of the Chibok girls. This BBOG executive therefore wanted the girls released from the Presidential Villa and not from the Sambisa forest. If this was an unfortunate slip of tongue by a garrulous female, there was worse to come.

A chieftain of the opposition APC made an all-time gaffe when he stated in a rally that "We commend the Bring Back Our Girls movement led by members of this party. We thank them for their commitment to Nigeria We hear that the federal government wants to take them to court. Let the courtroom be large enough to accommodate all of us when they sue them". The APC chieftain in question is Audu Innocent Ogbeh a former national Chairman of the ruling People's Democratic Party PDP. The man has since apologized to the BBOG movement for making this statement. His exact words were: "I feel obliged to let you know that my statement at our function last week was not intended to paint your group as an APC sub-group. This is because, from what we know, less than 2% of the group members are our party members we value highly. The rest of you are not and may not even belong to any political association whatsoever. This is not to say that you have no right to be here if you choose to."

It is hard to figure out what Mr. Ogbeh was thinking when he made the statement linking the BBOG movement to the APC but the statement had immediate results. A number of respectable people in the BBOG movement were scandalized and well they might. Ms Modupe Ozolua, in particular, parted ways with the movement because it became clear to her that the movement "had been politicized".

Modupe Ozolua comes across as a forthright person so it makes sense to quote her in full. On November 1, 2014 this lady appeared on the program Gender Agenda on African Independent Television (AIT). Speaking to Adaora Onyechere, the anchor of Gender Agenda, Ozolua stated: "I went to the first Bring Back Our Girls campaign. As far as I was concerned, it was a protest against what Boko Haram had done. It was not against the president and it was not against the government. I mean President Jonathan did not go to Chibok to kidnap those girls. Unfortunately, a particular group of people hijacked the Bring Back Our Girls movement. The whole thing has been politicized so I never went there again".

It is hard to know if the supporters of this movement outside Nigeria are aware that the BBOG movement has been hijacked by the opposition APC. It is also hard to tell if most of the members of this movement "are not APC members" as Mr Ogbeh stated. What we do know is that some people have decided to use the misfortune of the Chibok girls as an opportunity to score cheap political points and that is really sad. The opinion of the writers of this book is that some things are scared and human beings ought to have dignity and compassion. To see the misfortune of the Chibok girls as nothing but an opportunity for politicking is the height of callousness.

Chapter 9

The Idriss Deby Ceasefire

On October 17, 2014, Alex Badey and Mike Omeri called a press conference and made a startling announcement. Boko Haram had just signed a ceasefire with the federal government. Nigerian soldiers were directed to halt all on-going hostilities against the sect because other modalities of the ceasefire would be ironed out in due course. For those who do not know, Air Chief Marshal Alex Badey is the Chief of Defense Staff of Nigeria's armed forces. Mike Omeri is the Coordinator of the National Information Center. These are serious-minded men who do not have a reputation for making inaccurate announcements but we will get back to this point later.

The mood in Nigeria after this announcement can only be described as ecstatic. Ceasefire with Boko Haram meant the return of peace to northern Nigeria and the release of the Chibok girls. It also meant that millions of internally displaced people (who had become refugees in their own country) could finally return home. To the gallant military officers fighting the insurgency, peace was a welcome development, too. Repentant Boko Haram members had a huge stake in the ceasefire as well. The return of peace to Nigeria's troubled northeast meant many things to many people, but all Nigerians agreed that this was the best piece of news they had had in years. When this ceasefire turned out to be a sham, the sense of outrage and disappointment across the land was palpable.

There are vital questions here and none of them are easy to answer.

Was President Jonathan playing politics with the BH ceasefire and the release of the Chibok girls? According to the opposition All Progressives Congress, the answer is a resounding yes. However, anybody with eyes in his head can see that the APC has been less than honest in analyzing the Jonathan administration and the President's handling of the Boko Haram insurgency.

Did the Boko Haram High Command outsmart the Nigerian government? The thinking in certain quarters is that Boko Haram was losing the war and needed a breathing space badly so the so-called ceasefire was hurriedly "arranged" to give them some time to regroup. If this is true, it leaves another big question unanswered. Why did the Nigerian military accept a ceasefire when a military victory was clearly within reach?

Was President Jonathan a victim in this whole ceasefire saga? In other words, did certain people who are out to ridicule his government take him for a ride?

More to the point, what was the true role of Idriss Deby in all this? Idriss Deby Itno is the president of Chad, Nigeria's neighbor to the northeast. The man is a former rebel leader and a former military officer to boot. Did he act in good faith or was he out to put one over his Nigerian neighbors?

Clearly, there are no pat answers here and the writers of this book cannot pretend to have all the answers. Still, it is important to take a position on some of the issues raised above.

Was Mr. Jonathan playing politics with the ceasefire?

People who accuse the Nigerian president of playing politics with the ceasefire have made a connection between the timing of the ceasefire and the declaration of the president to seek re-election. The timing of the two events is just too convenient to be a coincidence. This may be true but the more important question here is simply this: Did Mr. Jonathan have an opportunity for a real ceasefire in the past? Did he ignore or postpone this opportunity until the perfect time?

Did the Boko Haram High Command outsmart the Nigerian government? From every indication, there is only one answer to this question and that is, "yes". Before the arrangement of the amnesty, the Nigerian military had a definite advantage in the war against the BH. A number of senior BH commanders had been killed and many BH foot soldiers had surrendered to gallant federal troops. It is safe to assume that Abubakar Shekau was running out of commanders and needed more time to regroup and re-strategize. If this is true, how could Shekau have predicted the botched amnesty correctly? Now, this is where things get a bit murky. Even after extensive research by both writers, there is no evidence to suggest that Idriss Deby colluded with Shekau to dupe the Nigerian government so we have to be honest here. The fact that the botched amnesty favored a certain Imam Abubakar Shekau does not mean that he orchestrated the whole drama. It is possible that a different party swindled the Nigerian government. If that other party is not Shekau or Idriss Deby, then who is the bad guy in this context? This is a crucial question and it will be answered in due course.

Was President Jonathan a victim in this whole ceasefire saga?

There is only one obvious answer here. Mr. Jonathan was the victim and not the villain in this saga. It is possible that some people misled the Nigerian president. It is also possible that his retinue of advisers and special assistants did not give him the right advice. Another likely explanation is that his desperation for a peace in the northeast made him believe in the ceasefire without checking everything out thoroughly. As the Executive President of Nigeria, Mr. Jonathan has to take the blame because under his watch, the giant of Africa ended up with egg on its face.

Chapter 10

What was the True Role of Idriss Deby in all This?

There are those who believe that Mr. Deby was out to embarrass the Nigerian government. The problem here is that it is very easy to make allegations but in criminal law, every accused person is considered innocent until a competent court finds him guilty. Does Idriss Deby have any reason to dupe the Nigerian government? No, he does not. Does Mr. Deby have anything to gain by promoting the BH agenda? Again, the answer is no. On the other hand the Chadian president has everything to lose by getting chummy with the BH leadership. Hanging out with suicide bombers and mass murderers can be a very dangerous business and this is something some power brokers in Nigeria have found out the hard way. Those who thought they could use the BH for their own selfish reasons have since discovered that they can no longer control the BH gunmen. The Hausa expression; "Bori ta karda boka" sums up the matter perfectly. This means that "the evil spirit has overcome the witch doctor". Let us hope that Idriss Deby is not the "boka" in this context.

If the Idriss Deby Amnesty is a scam, who is the scammer?

We have to make two vital assumptions here. Assumption No. 1, President Goodluck Jonathan is not guilty. Assumption No. 2, President Idriss Deby is not guilty. Now, this leaves a character called Danladi Ahmadu who goes by the impressive title of Chief Security Officer of the Boko Haram sect. This man definitely has questions to answer. Danladi Ahmadu made the ceasefire statement and below is the full text of that statement.

"I am Danladi Ahmadu and a member of the group and also working as Internal Chief Security Officer. Apart from security work, I am working as a senior advisor in the group. First I wish to explain to you to know that, Imam Shekau is not dead as claimed because recently there was even communication and so he is alive. On the girls that we took from Chibok, all that we want before we free the girls is to get justice from the Nigerian state because there are many of our members that their business premises were destroyed, some killed and others in detention and many other oppression. Our people under detention are too many and they did nothing and many of them are just ordinary members. The girls are fine, they are eating food and in good shape except challenges of reading in the camp. It is a lie that they are exposed to serial abuses, they are fine and in good health condition. All that we want to say is, it is not everything happening that is from us; some criminals are carrying their own act in the name of our group.

"Regarding the cease fire, we are talking and it will continue when some people deeply involved are back from their trips. We are discussing with Nigerian government and it is one Hassan that is leading the team. He is directly working with Nigerian President and we will continue talking when our own people return. When it is clear the girls will be free and the world will see. By the special grace of God we have cease fire and by the grace of God we will in the future create avenue and people will hear it directly from our leader, Imam Shekau".

Chapter 11

Reactions to the Ceasefire Statement

As soon as this statement became public, there were reactions from different places. Most ordinary Nigerians celebrated the ceasefire announcement and well they might. After almost six years of war, Nigerians were weary and were praying for an end to the war. However, one person who had close contact with the BH in the past was not impressed. His name is Ahmad Salkida, Nigerian journalist (from the restive northeast) who now lives in Dubai.

Salkida dismissed Danladi Ahmadu as an impostor and challenged him (Danladi Ahmadu) to a debate. According to Salkida, Mr. Danladi Ahmadu could not be a true member of the BH because his name, Danladi, is a name usually given to people born on Sunday. According to Salkida the name "Danladi" is filthy to the BH so it is very unlikely that anybody representing the sect will ever have a name like that.

Another person who did not believe in the ceasefire is Comrade Shehu Sani the Kaduna-based civil rights activist. According the Leadership Newspaper of October 20 2014, Comrade Sani, the president of Civil Rights Congress of Nigeria described the ceasefire as a scam. Sani went on to say that, either the federal government is being scammed or it is part of the scam. Mr. Sani pointed out that Danladi Ahmadu referred to the Jama'atul Ahlus Sunna Liddawati wal Jihad as Boko Haram. This is something no self-respecting member of the sect would ever do. Sani dismissed Danladi Ahmadu as a fraud and added that anybody who wants authentic information on the BH should contact Ahmad Salkida because this man is the best source for credible information on the Boko Haram.

Chapter 12

The Emergence of the Female Suicide Bomber

Many people in Nigeria have linked the emergence of the female suicide bomber to the kidnapping of the Chibok Girls. Some people have stated that some of the kidnapped girls are the ones being used by the Boko Haram commanders to carry suicide missions. It is hard to tell if this is true or not. What the writers of this book know for a fact is that most of the female suicide bombers are within the same age bracket as the kidnapped Chibok Girls. Again, there was no incident of bombing by female teenage girls before the kidnapping of the Chibok Girls.

Boko Haram Attacks by Female Suicide Bombers 2014-2015

1) **JUNE 8 2014** A middle aged lady arrives at a military barracks in Gombe, north eastern Nigeria. She detonated an explosive device killing herself and a nearby policeman. This lady was Nigeria's first official female suicide bomber.

2) **July 27 201** A female teenager blew herself up at a university campus in Kano. Five people were seriously injured in the blast.

3) **July 28 2014** A young lady at a gas station in Hotoro, a suburb of Kano joined a kerosene queue. The lady detonated an explosive device killing herself and four people and injuring 16 others.

4) **July 28 2014** A female teenager at a shopping center in Kano detonates a bomb killing herself and injuring six other people.

5) **July 30 2014** A female teenager blows herself up a crowded college campus in Kano killing herself and seven other people.

6) **December 10 2014** Two female suicide bombers detonate explosive devices in two separate attacks at the busy Kwari market in Kano. At least four people were killed in the twin attack.

7) **January 10 2015** A ten year old girl blew herself up in the north eastern city of Maiduguri in Borno state. 19 people were killed in the blast and there are indications that the girl acted against her will.

8) **January 11 2015** Two female suicide bombers believed to be aged 10-11 killed themselves and killed three other people at a market in Potiskum in Yobe state.

9) **February 22, 2015** A female suicide bomber detonates a bomb at the Potiskum mobile phone market killing herself and four others. Many other people were injured in the blast.

10) **March 1 2015** Two female suicide bombers kill themselves and two others in an attack in Maiduguri.

Chapter 13

Divided Opinions

It may not be correct to state that all the female suicide bombers listed above were girls kidnapped from the Government Girls Secondary School, Chibok. But there is definitely a connection between the kidnapping and the advent of the female suicide bomber. First, the Boko Haram leader Abubakar Shekau stated that the Chibok girls have converted to Islam and are now ready to "do the work commanded by Allah". Going by the weird logic of Abubukar Shekau, "the work commanded by Allah" may well include wearing an explosives belt and bombing the enemies of Islam. There is also the fact that there was no incident of suicide bombing by female insurgents in Nigeria until the Chibok girls were kidnapped by Shekau and his gang.

Another significant fact is that some of the girls carrying out these suicide missions may have done so against their will. A would-be suicide bomber in Kano revealed that the girls she followed to a certain location were not told what they would do when they got there. They were given mobile phones and instructed to call a particular number once they arrived at the location. It is likely that the explosives were remotely detonated by a different person once the girls had made the call.

Another popular opinion is that some of these girls are close relations of Boko Haram commanders who are eager to please their fathers, brothers and uncles by carrying out suicide missions for them. In the case of Kano, the female bombers were orphans and widows who were motivated by a sense of revenge. A military expert in Kano pointed out something that many people may have overlooked. According to this officer, Boko Haram now has an active female wing and female suicide bombers serve in this wing of the BH. This officer added that one Hafsat Usman Bako was a senior recruiting agent for Boko Haram. According the officer, Hafsat (who is now under arrest) is the widow of one Usman Bako, a BH fighter who was killed by Nigerian soldiers in Adamawa state.

Chapter 14

A Common Guilt is All We Share

The kidnapping of the Chibok girls and the fact that these girls seem to have disappeared off the face of the earth is one of the most terrible things that has ever happened to Nigeria. It may not quite be on the same scale as the bloody coup of January 1966 when about 30 political and military leaders from northern and western Nigeria were decimated (plus one eastern Nigerian colonel). It may not be as gruesome as the savage revenge coup of July 1966 when over 200 officers and men from Nigeria's eastern region were murdered. It may not be as gruesome as the genocide that was carried out by northern Nigerians on the people of the former eastern region in July 1966-October 1966. The Chibok girls may not share the same fate (we still hope the girls will return) with hundreds of Nigerians in Jos, Kaduna, Yelwa-Shendam, Zangon Kataf and Kano. In these places normal people like you and I went to work, to school and to the market and ended up in mass graves like animals. For all that, the kidnapping of the Chibok girls was a terrible thing in its own right.

What are the facts of the matter?

276 girls were snatched from a government secondary school in Chibok, Borno state in April 2014

It is now April, 2015 and the girls have not yet been rescued. Worse still, all attempts to rescue the girls have been fruitless so far. Some of the girls who escaped from their captors have terrible tales to tell. To compound the felony, the same people who kidnapped these innocent girls have gone ahead to kidnap more boys and girls from the same region and nothing has been done to stop them. Take it or leave it, this is the terrible reality of life in some parts of Nigeria today.

There is no point in sugar-coating things here. It is time to tell the truth, the whole truth and nothing but the truth. 276 Nigerian girls went to school to learn and prepare for the future. While they were preparing for their final examinations, a band of armed men invaded their school, burnt down their hostels and abducted all the girls. And the most terrible part of the tragedy is that Nigerians have not come together to fight this horrific injustice. Instead, the kidnapping of the Chibok girls has become an opportunity for hypocrisy, grandstanding and self righteous pontification by certain elements in the land.

In the ruling People's Democratic Party (PDP), the initial reaction by some people close to President Goodluck Jonathan was that there was no kidnapping. According to these people, the girls were simply hidden away by some members of the opposition party to embarrass Mr. Jonathan.

The conduct of some members of the opposition All Progressives Congress (APC) was not much better than that of those in the PDP. Some APC chieftains tried to blame Mr. Jonathan for the kidnapping of the Chibok girls and one party official went as far as stating that the president should not contest for re-election until he has rescued the kidnapped girls.

In the deep south of Nigeria, many people are guilty of insensitivity. Some unfortunate and uninformed people see the kidnapping of the Chibok girls as "northerners kidnapping fellow northerners". Clearly, this is a terrible and narrow-minded reaction to a national tragedy.

The Nigerian Army, the Nigeria Police and the Directorate of State Security (secret service) are guilty as well. If these agencies had done their work the right way, the Chibok girls would not have been kidnapped in the first place. The country's growing army of Boko Haram negotiators and Boko Haram consultants are guilty of grand deception. Investigations have shown that some of these people who claim to have a mandate from Abubakar Shekau have never met the man. Some Boko Haram consultants have collected millions of naira from the government officials by dangling the carrot of a BH ceasefire before a desperate Goodluck Jonathan administration.

Finally, the writers of this book cannot get away with a John-the-Baptist mentality. We simply cannot dole out generous portions of blame to other parties without admitting that we are blameworthy in some ways. If only we had done more.....If only we had alerted more people to the dangers the Boko Haram Sect posed to our society. If only we had started writing earlier than we did. If only we had spent more time in Yobe and Borno states (one of us, at least) investigating and reporting. In retrospect, there are too many "ifs" but in the final analysis, one thing is clear.

Concerning the tragedy that befell the Chibok girls, in Nigeria and beyond, before and after the kidnapping, a common guilt is all we share.

Chapter 15

The Ideology of the Boko Haram Sect

The Boko Haram sect calls itself Jama'atu Ahlus Sunna Lidda'awati Wal-Jihad and this means people committed to the propagation of the teachings of the Prophet and Jihad. Why are these people described as Boko Haram in Nigeria and beyond? The truth is that the leader of the group Muhammad Yusuf had a habit of describing westernization as haram (forbidden). According to Mr. Yusuf, democracy is haram. Working for the Nigerian civil service is haram and having boys and girls in the same high school is haram. In time, the man's repeated ranting that anything western is haram gave his organization the name Boko Haram.

Apparently, millions of Muslims in Nigeria did not share Yusuf's belief that Boko (western education) is haram. Below is a transcribed video debate between Muhammad Yusuf and Ustaz Idris Abdulaziz. Abdulaziz is the leader of the Jama'at Izalatul Al Bidiah Wa Ikamat Al-Sunnah. (Society of Removal of Innovation and Re-establishment of the Sunnah). This is a prominent Islamic organization with millions of followers in most parts of northern Nigeria.

Below is the transcribed video interview (unedited)

Ustaz Idris Abdulaziz: Is western as taught in our modern schools haram (forbidden) or halal (not forbidden).

Muhammad Yusuf: Islam looks at any form of knowledge in three ways. Any form of knowledge that has 100% compliance with Islam is halal and can even be wajib (compulsory). Any form that clashes with Islam is haram and can lead to shirk (disbelief). And any form that neither conforms nor clashes with Islam can neither be haram nor halal.

Ustaz Abdulaziz: I want you to give me a categorical answer. Is book haram or halal?

Muhammad Yusuf: Western education as taught in the kinds of schools we have in Nigeria is haram.

Ustaz Abdulaziz: Please give reasons from the Qur'an and Hadith in support of your assertion.

Muhammad Yusuf: (recites some verses from the Qur'an). There are aspects of western education as taught in our schools that make it haram. The mixing of opposite sexes makes it haram. The importance given to some non-Muslim days in the school calendar (Saturday, being Jewish holiday and Sunday being Christian holiday) also makes it haram. Allah in the Holy Qur'an said He created man from clay but its disputation by evolutionary theory makes it haram even bordering on shirk. And, the claim in western education that there are nine planets contradicts what Allah says, thereby making it haram."

Chapter 16

The Final interview

The former leader of Boko Haram was arrested by the military on July 30, 2009. He was handed over to the police but he died in police custody. Below is a transcribed video interview that is effectively the final interview of Muhammad Yusuf.

Military Officer: We went to your house yesterday and we saw a lot of animals, syringes and materials used for making bombs. What were you keeping all that for?

Muhammad Yusuf: Like I told you, to protect myself...

Military Officer: (cuts in) ... To protect yourself, how? Isn't there the authority, the law enforcement agencies?

Muhammad Yusuf: The authorities, the law enforcement agents are the same people fighting me.

Military Officer: What did you do?

Muhammad Yusuf: I don't know what I did ... I am only propagating my religion, Islam.

Military Officer: But I am also a Muslim like you.

Muhammad Yusuf: I don't know why you refuse to accept my own (Islam).

Military Officer: Why do you say Boko is haram?

Muhammad Yusuf: Of course, it is haram.

Military Officer: Why do you say that?

Muhammad Yusuf: The reasons are so many...

Military Officer: The trousers you are wearing...

Muhammad Yusuf: (cuts in) ... It is pure cotton and cotton belongs to Allah.

Military Officer: But, Allah said in the Qur'an; "Iqrah" (read) that people should seek knowledge...

Muhammad Yusuf: That is correct but not knowledge that contravenes the teachings of Islam. All knowledge that contradicts Islam is prohibited by the Almighty. Sihiri (sorcery or magic) is knowledge but Allah has forbidden it. Shirk (polytheism or sharing or associating partners to Allah) is knowledge but Allah has forbidden it...

Military Officer: At your place, we found computers, syringes, and so on. Are they not products of knowledge?

Muhammad Yusuf: They are purely technological things. Not Boko...and westernization is different.

Military officer: How come you are eating good food – look at you looking healthy – you are driving good cars and wearing good clothes while you are forcing your followers to sell their belongings and live mostly on dabino (dates) and water?

Muhammad Yusuf: That is not true. Everybody is living according to his means. Even you are different. Whoever you see driving cars, it is because he can afford them. And whoever you see living in want, it also means he doesn't have the wherewithal.

Military Officer: Why did you abandon your mosque and compound?

Muhammad Yusuf: Because you went there and opened fire there...

Military Officer: But you sent your people there to die in the fire.

Muhammad Yusuf: No, my people have left the place.

Military Officer: What about those who came to fight for you? Where and where do you have followers?

Muhammad Yusuf: You have chased all of them away.

Military Officer: Apart from Maiduguri...

Muhammad Yusuf: There are some in Bauchi but police chased them away. There are some in Yola, Adamawa – police attacked them. Same with those in Jalingo, Taraba state. It was after chasing them away that they turned to us here in Maiduguri.

Military Officer: What happened to your hand?

Muhammad Yusuf: I fell.

Military Officer: How many areas do you control in Maiduguri?

Muhammad Yusuf: The headquarters is right here.

Military Officer: What about other branches?

Muhammad Yusuf: We have in Gwange, bulunkutu…

Military Officer: (cuts in) …Where they intercepted weapons?

Muhammad Yusuf: (laughs) Intercepted weapons.

Military Officer: What about your 2i/c (second in command) … because they said you have soldiers, police, e.t.c.

Muhammad Yusuf: That is not true.

Military officer: But, don't you have a 2i/c who acts in your absence?

Muhammad Yusuf: I have.

Military Officer: What is his name?

Muhammad Yusuf: Malam Abubakar Shekau.

Military Officer: Where is he now?

Muhammad Yusuf: I don't know.

Military Officer: Who and who escaped with you?

Muhammad Yusuf: I did not run away with anybody.

Military Officer: Where are your sponsors, here at home or abroad?

Muhammad Yusuf: Nobody.

Military Officer: No, tell us the truth...

Muhammad Yusuf: Insha Allah, (by God's grace) I will not lie to you.

Military Officer: You have a farm in Benisheikh.

Muhammad Yusuf: Yes.

Military Officer: Now, you have made us kill people who are innocent. What do you have to say?

Muhammad Yusuf: You bear responsibility for those you killed.

Military Officer: What about those killed by your followers?

Muhammad Yusuf: My followers did not kill anybody.

Military Officer: What about those killed among your followers?

Muhammad Yusuf: Those killed among my followers, whoever killed them are the people who committed crimes.

Military Officer: Where are you from originally?

Muhammad Yusuf: I hail from Yobe state.

Military Officer: Where in Yobe state?

Muhammad Yusuf: Jakusko.

Military Officer: What about your father?

Muhammad Yusuf: He is from Jakusko.

Military Officer: What about your mother?

Muhammad Yusuf: She is from Gashua.

Military Officer: Have you ever travelled abroad?

Muhammad Yusuf: Only Hajj (pilgrimage to Makkah, Saudi Arabia)

Military Officer: What year was that?

Muhammad Yusuf: 2003 and 2004.

This interview is effectively the final testament of Ustaz Muhammad Yusuf. Some hours after he was handed over to the police, Muhammad Yusuf was reported dead. His deputy Abubakar Shekau took over and became the Amir ul-Aam (Commander-in Chief). It was under Shekau's regime that the bombing campaigns, drive-by shootings and large-scale kidnapping became standard book Haram policies.

A Word to Good Muslims

All over the world, good Muslims are always reluctant to condemn a fellow Muslim or pass a negative judgment on a fellow Muslim. Now, considering what Muhammad Yusuf and Abubakar Shekau have done to fellow Muslims (ummat al-Islamiyah) and to Christians (Ahl-ul-Kitaab), we have to wonder. If Muhammad Yusuf and Abubakar Shekau were good Muslims, one can only say; "Inna Lillahi Wa Inna Ilaihi Raji'un" It means from "Allah we came and to Allah we return."

Epilogue

Early Days of Boko Haram in Borno

It was a Sunday afternoon
And the location was Gwange Ward
In the heart of Maiduguri.

Pastor James parked his car
Under a neem tree and made
For the home of his friend, Ali.
They had been roommates
In the university of Maiduguri
But had lost contact after graduation.

Somehow, the place looked different
But he recognized some landmarks
And decided he was in the right place.
He felt eyes of hostility on him and turned
In time to see three youths armed with swords.

The silent trio grabbed him and
Wrestled him to the ground
Two of them held him down
While the third slit his throat.

One horrified neighbor turned
To his friend who had also witnessed
The gruesome cold-blooded murder.

“Did you see that?
They just slaughtered a man”.

“I saw nothing”, he replied
“And neither did you”.

Silently, both men sneaked into their homes
And locked the doors behind them.

Notes

Chapter 1

The government official in chapter 1 prefers not to be mentioned by name. The soldier he spoke to also prefers that his identity be withheld.

Chapter 2

The "Ika" people are also called Ika Igbo. They are closely related to the Igbo people of south eastern Nigeria and most Ika people speak Igbo but they also have their own dialects.

"Ladi Ndiribula" is not the real name of the lady mentioned in Chapter 2. Ladi is a very common name in the Christian areas of northern Nigeria. It is the name given to female children born on Sunday. "Nidiribula" is also a common Chibok name.

Chapter 3

Mrs. Asabe Kwambura is the real name of the Principal of the school from which the girls were kidnapped.

Chapter 5

"Bush, Obama and Jonathan..." The enemies of Islam that Shekau named in the said video are Barak Obama and George W. Bush, present and former presidents of the USA. Goodluck Ebele Jonathan is Nigeria's current president.

Malam Aminu Kano was a prominent Nigerian politician. He was the founder of the Northern Elements Progressives Union (NEPU) in Nigeria's first republic. He was also founder and presidential candidate of the Peoples Redemption Party (PRP) during Nigeria's second republic. He championed the rights of oppressed people in northern Nigeria and is considered a hero in Kano and other parts of northern Nigeria. Sir Abubakar Tafawa Balewa was Nigeria's first Prime-Minister. In Shekau's opinion, these illustrious Nigerians were enemies of Islam because they participated in the democratic process. Usman Dan Fodio was the leader of the Sokoto Jihad and the founder of the Sultanate in present day Nigeria.

Shendam and Zangon Kataf are towns in Plateau and Kaduna states of north central Nigeria. In both places, hundreds of Muslims were killed in reprisal killings by local Christian tribesmen.

Chapter 7

Gen. Mathew Olusegun Obasanjo is the only Nigerian who has ruled the country as military Head of State (1976-1979) and as a civilian president (1999-2007). The man is noted for his sharp tongue and unapologetic bluntness. When he made the famous declaration that the "girls may never return", many people condemned him for being pessimistic but a few people felt he was just being honest and realistic.

Chapters 9-11

In February 2015, President Goodluck Jonathan finally cleared the air on the Idris Deby ceasefire. In a presidential media chat televised by the Nigeria Television Authority (NTA), on February 11 2015, Mr. Jonathan effectively passed a vote of confidence on Mr. Idris Deby. According to Goodluck Jonathan, nobody was swindled. The Nigerian government saw a window of opportunity and tried to act on the information in good faith. Unfortunately, it turned out that Boko Haram has different factions and the government was dealing with the wrong faction.

Almad Salkida and Shehu Sani have to be commended here. When they stated that Danladi Ahmadu might be an impostor, many people in Nigeria wanted to lynch them for being cynical and pessimistic. As it turned out, everything the duo said about Ahmadu and the so-called ceasefire has been spot on.

Chapter 16

Ummat al-islamiyah means the community of believers and refers to all Muslims in the world. Ahl-ul-Kitaab simply means "people of the book". Christians and Jews are considered people of the book because they are guided by their own religious books and they practice monotheism.

References

http://africacheck.org/factsheets/factsheet-how-many-schoolgirls-did-boko-haram-abduct-and-how-many-are-still-missing/

http://www.punchng.com/news/lt-col-15-others-to-face-trial-over-chibok-girls/

http://www.bbc.com/news/world-africa-27283383

http://www.vanguardngr.com/2014/05/chibok-kidnap-scam-says-asari-dokubo/

http://dailypost.ng/2014/10/06/chibok-girls-may-never-return-others-will-produce-babies-boko-haram-members-obasanjo/

http://www.punchng.com/news/boko-haram-holding-165-chibok-christian-girls-can/

http://www.thisdaylive.com/articles/chibok-can-releases-names-of-180-abducted-schoolgirls/177814/

http://saharareporters.com/2014/10/19/boko-haram%E2%80%99s-%E2%80%9Crepresentative%E2%80%9D-ceasefire-talks-bogus-says-salkida

List of Kidnapped Chibok Girls

Below is the list of Kidnapped Chibok girls released by the Christian Association of Nigeria (CAN) and published by THISDAY NEWSPAPER on May 5, 2014.

Abducted Chibok Girls

Christian Girls

1 Deborah Abge Chrstian
2. Awa Abge
3. Hauwa Yirma
4. Asabe Manu
5. Mwa Malam Pogu
6. Patience Dzakwa
7. Saraya Mal. Stover
8. Mary Dauda
9. Gloria Mainta
10. Hanatu Ishaku
11. Gloria Dama
12. Tabitha Pogu
13. Maifa Dama
14. Ruth Kollo
15. Esther Usman
16 Awa James
17 Anthonia Yahonna
18 Kume Mutah
19 Aisha Ezekial
20 Nguba Buba
21 Kwanta Simon
22 Kummai Aboku
23 Esther Markus
24 Hana Stephen
25. Rifkatu Amos
26 Rebecca Mallum
27. Blessing Abana
28. Ladi Wadai
29. Tabitha Hyelampa
30 Ruth Ngladar
31 Safiya Abdu
32 Naomi Yahonna
33 Solomi Titus
34 Rhoda John
35 Rebecca Kabu

36. Christy Yahi
37. Rebecca Luka
38. Laraba John
39 Saratu Markus
40. Mary Usman
41. Debora Yahonna
42. Naomi Zakaria
43. Hanatu Musa
44. Hauwa Tella
45. Juliana Yakubu
46. Suzana Yakubu
47. Saraya Paul
48. Jummai Paul
49. Mary Sule
50. Jummai John
51. Yanke Shittima
52. Muli Waligam
53. Fatima Tabji
54. Eli Joseph
55. Saratu Emmanuel
56. Deborah Peter
57. Rahila Bitrus
58. Luggwa Sanda
59. Kauna Lalai
60. Lydia Emmar
61. Laraba Maman
62. Hauwa Isuwa
63. Comfort Habila
64. Hauwa Abdu
65. Hauwa Balti
66. Yana Joshua
67. Laraba Paul
68. Saraya Amos
69. Glory Yaga
70. Naomi Bitrus
71. Godiya Bitrus
72. Awa Bitrus
73. Na'omi Luka
74. Maryamu Lawan
75. Tabitha Silas
76. Mary Yahona
77. Ladi Joel
78. Rejoice Sanki
79. Luggwa Samuel
80. Comfort Amos
81. Saraya Samuel

82. Sicker Abdul
83. Talata Daniel
84. Rejoice Musa
85. Deborah Abari
86. Salomi Pogu
87. Mary Amor
88. Ruth Joshua
89. Esther John
90. Esther Ayuba
91. Maryamu Yakubu
91. Zara Ishaku
93. Maryamu Wavi
94. Lydia Habila
95. Laraba Yahonna
96. Naomi Bitrus
97. Rahila Yahanna
98. Ruth Lawan
99. Ladi Paul
100. Mary Paul
101. Esther Joshua
102. Helen Musa
103. Margret Watsai
104. Deborah Jafaru
105. Filo Dauda
106. Febi Haruna
107. Ruth Ishaku
108. Racheal Nkeki
109. Rifkatu Soloman
110. Mairama Yahaya
111. Saratu Dauda
112. Jinkai Yama
113. Margret Shettima
114. Yana Yidau
115. Grace Paul
116. Amina Ali
117. Palmata Musa
118. Awagana Musa
119. Pindar Nuhu
120. Yana Pogu
121. Saraya Musa
122. Hauwa Joseph
123. Hauwa Kwakwi
125. Hauwa Musa
126. Maryamu Musa
127. Maimuna Usman
128. Rebeca Joseph

129. Liyatu Habitu
130. Rifkatu Yakubu
131. Naomi Philimon
132. Deborah Abbas
133. Ladi Ibrahim
134. Asabe Ali
135. Maryamu Bulama
136. Ruth Amos
137. Mary Ali
138. Abigail Bukar
139. Deborah Amos
140. Saraya Yanga
141. Kauna Luka
142. Christiana Bitrus
143. Yana Bukar
144. Hauwa Peter
145. Hadiza Yakubu
146. Lydia Simon
147. Ruth Bitrus
148. Mary Yakubu
149. Lugwa Mutah
150. Muwa Daniel
151. Hanatu Nuhu
152. Monica Enoch
153. Margret Yama
154. Docas Yakubu
155. Rhoda Peter
156. Rifkatu Galang
157. Saratu Ayuba
158. Naomi Adamu
159. Hauwa Ishaya
160. Rahap Ibrahim
162. Deborah Soloman
163. Hauwa Mutah
164. Hauwa Takai
165. Serah Samuel

Muslim Girls

166. Aishatu Musa
167. Aishatu Grema
168. Hauwa Nkeki
169. Hamsatu
Abubakar

170. Mairama
Abubakar
171. Hauwa Wule
172. Ihyi Abdu
173. Hasana Adamu
174. Rakiya Kwamtah
175. Halima Gamba
176. Aisha Lawan
177. Kabu Malla
178. Yayi Abana
179. Falta Lawan
180. Kwadugu Manu

ISBN-13: 978-1508907541
ISBN-10: 1508907544

www.ingramcontent.com/pod-product-compliance
Lightning Source LLC
Chambersburg PA
CBHW070505290526
45790CB00003B/1100

* 9 7 8 1 5 0 8 9 0 7 5 4 1 *